According to Celtic
legend, hazelnuts give
knowledge and wisdom.

The Apple Tree Man
lives in the oldest tree
in every orchard.

# Fairy rings

A bright green ring on the grass or a circle of toadstools is said to be a fairy ring, where fairies dance on summer nights. Humans, however, should beware. Legends tell of people joining in a fairy dance only to discover, when it has ended, that many years have passed.

Thorn trees on a hill
mean it might be a
home to fairies.

# Goblin market

Fairy food is tempting but dangerous – those who eat it may never escape from Fairyland, or else die of longing to return. The poem, 'Goblin Market', by Christina Rossetti, carries the warning: 'We must not look at goblin men, We must not buy their fruits: Who knows upon what soil they fed, Their hungry thirsty roots?'

# Water fairies

From nixies in their streams, to merfolk and sea serpents in the oceans, water fairies appear in stories around the world, cursing with storms or blessing with treasure.

### Asrai
a Scottish water fairy who melts into a pool of water when caught in sunlight. The females have long, green hair and webbed feet.

### Shellycoat
a Scottish water fairy of freshwater streams. It is covered in shells and clatters as it moves.

### Nixie
a German freshwater fairy that is dangerous to humans, trapping their souls in lobster pots.

### Hotot
from Armenian folklore. Hotots always appear covered in mud and slime.

### Njuzu
a southern African water fairy, similar to a mermaid.

### Mermaids
fish-tailed women who try
to lure sailors with their
songs of enchantment.

### Nereid
a sea nymph of Greek
mythology, said to
protect sailors.

### Merrow
Irish merperson. The females look like
mermaids, but the males are green, with
webbed hands and fish-like faces.

### Sea trow
creature at the bottom of the sea,
that surfaces disguised as a seal.

# The end of a rainbow

Rainbows and fairies are often linked together. A leprechaun
stores his gold at the end of a rainbow, and in many myths
a rainbow is a bridge or ladder to another world.

If ever captured by a human, a leprechaun
has the magical power to grant three
wishes in exchange for his freedom.

To get a pot of gold away from a leprechaun, you must see him before he sees you.

Dwarfs mine for gold underground. They are also masters at crafting gold.

# Midsummer's Eve

At Midsummer, fairies are said to be at their most powerful. Old wives' tales tell of herbs collected on Midsummer's Eve having greater power for healing and magic. It is also a time for dancing and revelry.

Midsummer is the ancient celebration of the summer solstice, when the sun reaches its highest point in the sky.

Fairy instruments include fiddles, harps, pipes and cymbals. Their music is often described as sweet and wild.

According to legend,
anyone who hears fairy music
will never be the same again.

# Night sprites

Night time is fairy time, when fairy creatures are at their most active. Many stories about fairies grew out of people's fear of the dark, and all that might be lurking there...

Phookas are trickster fairies that change into horses to give wild, frightening rides.

A night-hag is an evil fairy that wanders through the darkness, giving people nightmares.

Will-o'-the-wisps hover in the darkness.

Night sprites can be good or bad. Some lead people astray; others light their way home.

# Finding fairies

Folklore tells of many ways to look for signs of fairies, from little burning globes in the night air to a ring of toadstools that marks a dancing place, or a field of wild flowers.

A field unusually thick with flowers can be a sign of fairy presence.

The toadstool most associated with fairies is Fly Agaric, which is red with white spots.

In Welsh legends, the way to fairy islands is marked by a tiny door in a rock, which leads to a secret passage beneath a lake.

After dark, look for little burning globes in the night sky.